12-7-07

2005 Indin.

Very Good

EDIT 121.

2013 Like New 28.00

KERALA
of Gods and Men

Johnathan Watts

KERALA
of Gods and Men

Introduction by Laurent Aubert

TIMELESS
BOOKS

This edition was first published in India in 2005 by
Timeless Books
46, Housing Society,
South Extension Part-1
New Delhi-110 049
Tel. : 2469 0513, 2469 3257
E-mail : timeless@satyam.net.in
Website : www.timelessartbooks.com

© Musée d'ethnographie, Geneva, 2004
© 5 Continents Editions srl, Milan, 2004

ISBN : 81-902369-6-2

Ethnographic Museum of Geneva

Editorial Coordinator
Geneviève Perret

Captions
Johnathan Watts, Geneviève Perret, Laurent Aubert

Translation
Isabelle Schulte-Tenckhoff

Map
Jean-Pierre Peney

5 Continents Editions

Editorial Coordinator
Laura Maggioni

Editing
Timothy Stroud

Design and Layout
Marina Longo

Colour separation
Eurofotolit, Cernusco sul Naviglio (Milan)

Printed in November 2004 by Bianca & Volta, Truccazzano
(Milan) for 5 Continents Editions, Milan – Italy

This book is published during the *Indian Seasons* in Geneva
for the exhibition «Kerala, the Flames of the Goddess» taking
place at the Ethnographic Museum of Geneva, from March 22
to December 31, 2005.

Acknowledgements

I am extremely indebted to: Ravi Gopalan Nair for his unique
and invaluable help in the field and his everlasting friendship,
Gopal Venu the director of the Natana Kairali Institute,
who has defended and supported the traditional theatre
of Kerala for so many years, Laurent Aubert my colleague from
the Ethnographic Museum and inspired travelling companion,
Geneviève Perret for her unwavering support in realising
this publication, Cendrine Hostettler for her precious help
in documenting and archiving the 7000 photographs taken
during the course of the two field trips, the Ethnographic
Museum of Geneva and the Society of the Friends of the
Ethnographic Museum of Geneva, and finally, to the
people and artists of Kerala.

Johnathan Watts

Table of contents

Note
Most of the names have been
transcribed from malayalam,
main spoken language of Kerala.

A Pact with the Gods

Laurent Aubert

The photography of Johnathan Watts allows us to share his regard on Kerala, a regard which was linked to my note taking and musical recordings during our two fieldtrips in 1998–99 and 2001. His vision shows images of a reality which it was my task to document. In our common wanderings, we were guided by intuition. We were always ready, should the opportunity arise, to respond to the entreaties of the gods and the people of Kerala. At each and every moment, our complicity was enhanced by the expert knowledge of our friend Ravi Gopalan Nair, who travelled with us throughout our missions. His understanding of the rituals of Kerala revealed to us their mysteries as they unfolded on our journey from village to village.

Having long been familiar with India, we knew that fieldwork in this region was hardly a trivial matter. Having determined to compare our experience with the lessons to be drawn from the field, we were conquered straightaway by a land of heady scents, landscapes with lush vegetation, towns and villages teeming with colourfully garbed but unobtrusive people, melodies monotonously transmitted by the temple loud-speakers, and, above all, by the innumerable and omnipresent gods and goddesses, the heroes and heroines of a parallel world the presence of which, though we were not fully aware of it, was fascinating to us.

Strongly present in the shrines devoted to them, in the images representing them, in the myths that speak about them and in the bodies of the dancers who incarnate them, the gods and goddesses of Kerala inhabit the thoughts, sustain the gestures of everyday life, and punctuate the rhythm of life.

As paradoxical entities, both terribly close and desperately distant, the gods and goddesses of Kerala are the sublimated doubles of those who worship them. Whether protective fathers or sympathetic mothers, dispensers of justice combating demons, mistresses of demanding ardour, tutelary spirits pulling wry faces, androgynous chimera or dubious mythical serpents, they offer numerous facets of the Invisible, of an elusive reality from which no one seeks to escape. As the supreme rulers of a society devoted to them, the gods of Kerala have all the rights and all the powers except, perhaps, the one that would allow them to choose not to be gods…

Like human beings, the deities of the pantheon cannot escape the fate determined by what Hinduism calls *dharma*, which is to say, Cosmic Law or Cosmic Order. Like human beings, the gods are its instruments and must therefore comply with the demands of those who invoke them through the appropriate rituals. Modest offerings made privately at the family altar, mysterious séances featuring spiritual possession guided by a specialist of the Beyond, or spectacular collective ceremonies in which the entire community takes part are all acts that punctuate the life cycle of the faithful and seem to derive almost naturally from a mysterious covenant with the gods and the spirits – a covenant whose clauses are agreed upon but whose benefits remain uncertain.

As providential tools and the keystone of the social order, rituals allow each individual to try to bend the will of the celestial beings, to urge them to manifest themselves, bringing with them their blessings. Sacrifices are gifts given meaning by the fact that they must be returned in the form of a special favour granted by the receiving deity. According to the rationale of this particular spiritual economy, the gods are no longer free once they have been appealed to. They are bound by an exchange they cannot avoid; using the powers vested in them, they must participate. The sacrifice, if properly conducted, thus turns out to be more powerful than the gods!

Rituals can only be efficient if they are planned and conducted with the purpose of seducing and attracting the gods by flattering their senses. Hence the capital importance of the aesthetic aspect of these events, whatever their scale. Nothing is too beautiful to arouse the benevolence of the gods: the loveliest images, the most refined music, the most complex rhythms, the most spectacular dances, the most delicious food… All these devices, all these generous gifts originate from a science of the Beyond, from a highly sophisticated skill and artistry, as Keralan culture shows with particular generosity.

By and large, most ceremonies take place at the shrines. Here, the traditional narratives are sung, the sacred diagrams are drawn, and many ritual dances are performed. Despite overall changes, modernity has had little impact on the form and substance of these events as they perpetuate the presence of the fundamental myths and archetypes. Although the shrines are lit nowadays by fluorescent lights rather than fire torches, they still serve as the backdrop to gods, heroes and ancestors embodied by eccentric looking characters. Richly decked out, these move to the thundering beat of the percussion that marks the transition from ordinary time to the sacred time of the ritual, to the out-of-time.

In Kerala, both rituals and the theatrical arts are part of a long cultural tradition. It is often difficult to distinguish between the ancient local civilisation, whether Dravidian or pre-Dravidian, and the Brahmanic culture of Aryan origin. One notes a constant symbiosis of both levels of Indian culture, which are often described as "high tradition" – classical India as it has evolved to this day – and "low tradition" – namely the vernacular cultures with their idiosyncrasies. In this manner, Indian culture as a whole bears witness to a constant back-and-forth between two opposing and complementary poles, a dialectics of "high" and "low" culture, of the global – at the level of India – and the local.

The arrival of Brahmanism was no threat to Keralan rituals, most of which are of indigenous origin. On the contrary, Brahmanism incorporated them by providing a framework that facilitated their development yet helped to preserve their autonomy and vitality. This attitude of tolerance explains why the villagers rarely reject Brahmanic authority. Though recognising this authority, they also claim their own place within it based on their hereditary attributes and individual qualities.

The complementary relationship between pan-Indian Brahmanism and local tradition is particularly manifest in Kerala. It is especially apparent in the religious beliefs and practices of the inhabitants, but also in the mythology and its many images.

The Hindu pantheon is presided over by three main deities: Brahmâ the Creator, Vishnu the Preserver, and Shiva the Destroyer (Shiva is also venerated as the master of time, the perfect ascetic and the king of the dance). Most other gods are either particular incarnations of these three deities or characters belonging to their offspring or following. The gods outside that category, such as Indra, Sûrya, Agni or Vâyu, are part of the ancient Vedic tradition that predates Brahmanism. Still other gods, like Ayyappan, Kuttichâtan and Muttappan, are of local origin.

The numerous female deities are generally the wives or daughters of the gods, but in symbolic terms they are all regarded as emanations of Mâhadevî, the "Great Goddess". As such, they represent the acting principle of Divinity, its power or energy (*shaktî*), from which the visible world originates. For this reason, the faithful often invoke one form or another of the Goddess, especially during Tantric rituals. In this spiritual tradition, which is most influential in Kerala, the Goddess is mysteriously present in the words and acts that evoke her, as well as in the persons, images and objects endowed with her power.

One characteristic of Tantrism is that it is, in principle, accessible to all, without distinction of caste or sex.

Contrary to the ascetic and contemplative traditions based on renouncing the world, Tantrism seeks to reconcile the spiritual aspirations of its followers and their enjoyment of worldly goods. The initiate remains active in society, albeit in an autonomous and detached fashion. He both dominates his own ego and the world in which he lives.

Many female deities venerated in Kerala are manifestations of Kâli, the "black one", a terrible and destructive form of the Goddess. The main manifestations are Bhagavatî, the "fortunate", "glorious" or "adorable" one, and Bhadrakâli, literally the "virtuous", "radiant" or "propitious" Kâli. But one also encounters other forms, such as Nâgakâli, the "Kâli with the serpents", Ottakkâli, the "Kâli with the bamboos", or Châmundî, who subjugated the demons Chanda and Munda. A local manifestation of the Goddess may be the object of a cult, as in the case of Muchilôttu-Bhagavatî, Narampil-Bhagavatî or Kannangâttu-Bhagavatî, who are named after the places in which they appeared. But these are all facets of the same female essence, beyond their many guises – whether the serene and benevolent protectress of order and justice or the terrifying, ferocious and destructive female warrior leading the charge against the army of demons.

Demons (*asura*) incarnate the tendencies of the inferior psyche. They belong to the transient world of the spirits, to the realm also peopled by ghosts (*bhûta*), genies (*yaksha* and *yakshî*), celestial musicians endowed with occult powers (*gandharva*), war heroes (*vîra*) and serpent-gods (*nâga*). Like the venom of the *nâga*, their powers contain an ambiguous energy. The initiate has to learn how to use it properly, like a drug that may either cure or kill.

The importance of the cult of the ancestors in Kerala must also be understood. Each family is bound to honour its ancestors, for they are part of the chain linking it to its origin. As guardians of the homes and masters of the pathways, the ancestors are always honoured by an altar in the family shrine. By calling on them to appear on Earth during rituals, the community seeks to reaffirm the ties of solidarity that join the world of the living to the world of the spirits.

Many of these more or less legendary characters are regarded as heroes or lower deities. Their common trait is their exceptional destiny and their often violent death. They are "living dead" for whom no proper funeral rites were conducted and whose souls are condemned to roam between the world of the living and the realm of the gods. For this reason, they must return periodically among humans to close the cycle of their earthly existence and carry out the acts required to ensure their deliverance from the cycle of rebirths that determines the existence of all living beings. Their main role is one of intercession and therapy. They protect their lineage against the type of malediction to which they themselves have fallen victim.

Every god, spirit and ancestor inhabiting the imagined world of Kerala personifies specific cosmic functions, qualities or determinations of being. Thus Hindu polytheism is only apparent, as each deity is but one aspect of "Divinity-as-such" to which he or she is ultimately assimilated. Each follower of Hinduism loosely defined chooses a "favourite deity" according to family tradition, initiation or personal preference, however, beneath the multiple layers of sensory form, he always venerates Divinity-as-such, which is unique and formless.

Religion and art constantly interact in the culture of Kerala – as is generally the case in Indian civilisation. The sacred manifests itself to varying degrees in all art forms, according to the function attributed to a given genre and to the event at which it is performed or of which it is a part. Indeed, there is an essential difference between a ritual conducted within a temple or consecrated place, and a worldly performance occurring outside, "in front of the temple" (*pro fano*), whose function and implications are of a profane order.

In this regard, Indian custom distinguishes between the two complementary categories of ritual arts and expressive arts. Ritual arts in the proper sense of the term are meant to materialise the presence of the divine in various forms. These may be either animate (in the body of an officiant or dancer, in the lyrics of a song or in the rhythm of a drum) or inanimate (in an image or object "inhabited" by the presence). Under the guise of entertainment, so-called "expressive arts" are performed to sharpen the senses and fulfil a didactic or moral function. A bawdy or farcical entertainment is therefore approached as a life lesson with its own symbols and teachings.

In this regard, nothing is further from the traditional Indian mind than the notion of *l'art pour l'art*. The artist's responsibility is not to express himself but to express what must be expressed by his art, according to the rules of his art. Artistic creation is never unmotivated: on the contrary, it is always the representation or imitation of a model or archetype whose presence, powers and precepts it is meant to bring out.

In the case of the ritual dances of Kerala mentioned above, which are splendidly illustrated by several pictures in the following pages, this presence is real: it is embodied by the dancer and brought to life by his movements, and hence expressed dynamically. The dancer is genuinely "visited" by the spirit of the deity, hero or ancestor he represents. The rituals of offering and invocation preceding the dance are meant to invite this entity to inhabit the dancer's body temporarily and to dissolve his conscience so that the entity can act within and through the dancer, carried along by sound of the oboes and drums. Once the dance is over, other rites are conducted with the purpose of bringing the entity to leave his human abode and return to the realm of the gods to allow the officiant to recover his normal state.

Conversely, in a play or the performance of a classical dance, the presence of the gods is not considered real but only suggestive: it is not a matter of possession but rather of representation. The actor plays his part lucidly, building up his role using the expressive means at his disposal. Fully aware of his effect on the public, he controls his performance at each moment. He knowingly applies the stylistic and symbolic codes of his art, which he uses according to his talent, his stage experience and, if applicable, his inspiration. When inspired and totally absorbed by his part, the actor undergoes an intense aesthetic experience that allows him to attain a temporary state of grace by internally perceiving and contemplating his character with its own emotions and feelings.

By and large, each dramatic genre in Kerala, whether of a ritual order or not, can be viewed as a total or synaesthetic performance that brings together a variety of expressive means, including speech, music, gesture, costume, make-up, accessories, and perfumes. All serve the same cause: to reaffirm the solidarity and interdependence of the world of the living and that of the gods and archetypes.

Keralan rituals, dramatic arts and dances thus plunge us into a timeless world. Their teachings touch upon the most universal and hence innermost dimension of being. The Western world has equivalents in the form of Greek tragedy or medieval mystery plays; but contrary to the West, India has managed to keep this tradition alive.

An outstanding trait of Keralan culture is the surprising diversity of its artistic and religious heritage. Each region, sometimes each village, has developed its own resources and its own specific ritual practices.

However, despite these proclaimed differences, one is also struck by the coherence of these multiple manifestations of the sacred, all propelled by the awareness of the same spiritual necessities and governed by a common idea about the place of the human being in the universe. One encounters the same mental structures, aesthetic codes and sources of reference and inspiration, albeit expressed by a prodigious multiplicity of forms and means.

Two major ritual traditions coexist in Malabar, the "land of hills" located in northern Kerala: the Teyyam or Teyyâttam (literally "dance of the gods"), which is widespread in the northern districts of Kannur and Kasaragod, and the Tirayâttam, the "dance of splendour" found in the region of Kozhikode (Calicut) further to the south. As their names indicate, these two genres focus on the idea that the gods and the ancestors really take up residence in the bodies of the dancers. This somewhat eucharistic appearance of the divine is celebrated with all the more pomp as each deity is endowed with special powers whose effects are meant to spread through the community of worshippers. The nature of these powers directly stems from the legend surrounding each god. It contributes to determining the choice of *teyyam* or *tira* performed on a given site. Some may allow a sterile couple to have a child, others provide a cure for smallpox, and yet others appease conflicts, bless the livestock and harvests, or chase away bad spirits negatively influencing an area of family dwellings.

To be efficient, the gods must be represented in a spectacular fashion. Their costumes, make-up and masks are aesthetically striking and the smallest detail is attended to with utmost care. The most spectacular element of the ceremonial garb is generally the headdress – sometimes reaching a height of six metres – from which the influence of the gods is meant to emanate. During the dances, the power of the gods can also be measured by the occasional atypical phenomenon: a *teyyam* wallowing in flames but complaining of the cold, another carrying a humanly impossible load, another appearing in two places at once: all these marvels bear witness to the reality of the powers at large.

The region extending from Ernakulam to Kottayam in central Kerala is home to the Mutiyêttu, a ritual performance recalling the combat between the goddess Bhadrakâli and the demon Dârikan. The term "Mutiyêttu" derives from *muti* ("hair" or "headdress") and *ettu* ("to carry"). It refers to the spectacular headdress worn by the actors, especially the one embodying the Goddess. The séance is always preceded by the drawing of the "*kalam*", an image of Bhadrakâli, with coloured powders on the ground. Although applied with particular skill and care, it is not meant to last: as soon as it is finished, it is wiped out ritually to make room for the living image of the Goddess in the person of the actor who represents her.

In many ways, the Mutiyêttu resembles a popular drama and thus differs fundamentally from the Teyyam or the Tirayâttam. In dramatizing a myth, the Mutiyêttu follows a storyline and is characterised by a properly theatrical structure, stage setting and dynamics. A genuine show, it involves astounding performances by actors with dazzling costumes and make-up, as well as gripping special effects. Yet the storyline is extremely simple since it recounts the elementary combat between Good and Evil and the inevitable victory, symbolised by the destruction of Dârikan, of the former. Herein lies the universality of the Mutiyêttu, as well as the cause of its ritual efficacy: albeit in archaic form, it is drama boiled down to its essentials, bringing into play the fundamental forces of the cosmos.

Another major Keralan ritual is the Patayani. This is celebrated each year in the village shrines in the districts of Alappuzha and Pathanamthitta, not far from the capital Trivandrum. The Patayani is the continuation of the Mutiyêttu in the "mythical chronology" of Kerala as it commemorates the triumph of the Goddess after her victory over the demon Dârikan. Organised as a large festival, this ceremony is a kind of direct confrontation between the community and the Goddess in the guise of Bhairavî – the "terrible one", according to another name of Bhadrakâli.

Each deity has his or her own form or *kôlam*, consisting of a headdress or mask made from arec leaves painted with symbols representing nature and its powers. The most spectacular is the *valiya-kôlam* ("grand *kôlam*") of Bhairavî, traditionally made of 1001 leaves sewn onto a huge wooden structure. On the opening night of the Patayani season, this structure, loaded onto a huge float drawn by at least two hundred men, is carried in a procession.

Devotion to the Goddess is central in the Patayani, but nevertheless linked to a form of "cult of nature" where trees, water, hills, thunder and lightning are viewed as divine manifestations which may either protect or destroy. In this regard, the Patayani tradition, centred around the principle of divine immanence, involves a form of pantheism. This distinguishes it from the idea of the sacred more closely related to Brahmanism, which has flowed into rituals such as the Teyyam, Tirayâttam or Mutiyêttu.

Rather than negating differences of caste and condition, the collective celebrations take these factors into account. At the same time, they are an opportunity for the most disadvantaged groups to assume particular value, notably when they take upon themselves the heavy task of embodying the gods and the ancestors. Following a process of compensatory inversion that we observed on many occasions, members of such groups, though traditionally relegated to the category of Untouchables, fulfil an essential priestly function. In this manner, they temporarily become equal to the Brahmans and spokespeople for the gods – a rare privilege indeed.

In this context, it is useful to address the issue of social organisation, which plays an important role in the unfolding of the rituals mentioned above. Indeed, their set-up involves many specialists, all with specific knowledge. Each of them is therefore an indispensable participant in the various stages of planning and conducting the ritual. Whatever their individual competence, all contribute to the whole according to their individual attributes, which are generally inherited on the basis of jealously guarded family traditions. By and large, these have remained the privilege of specific castes, sometimes even of particular lineages within the caste, and they constitute the raison d'être and often also a means of support for the group.

As a matter of principle, castes, which are a characteristic of India, have given rise to incomprehension and rejection among the vast majority of Westerners. Undoubtedly, a concept such as "untouchable" is shocking to us, and the basic inequality between the different communities that constitute Indian society is hardly compatible with the ideals of freedom and equality predominant in a modern democracy worthy of that name. But it would be futile to condemn without trying to understand, for otherwise one runs the risk of not grasping anything about the values characteristic of Indian civilisation and worldview.

The caste system can be approached theoretically – as an ideological principle of social hierarchy – and empirically – as an observable cultural reality resulting from a long process of evolution and adaptation. According to the model imposed by Brahmanism, in traditional hierarchical order the four major hereditary categories (*varna:* "colour", "varnish") of Indian society are: *brâhmana* (Brahmans, the priestly caste), *kshatriya* (warriors, leaders), *vaishya* (herders, farmers, artisans and traders) and *shûdra* (providers of services). The latter form the majority of the population in Kerala, as elsewhere in India. At the lowest end of the social ladder one finds the Untouchables (*asprshya*) or caste-less (*avarna*), who form the fifth collective in Hindu society. Many Untouchables, including the so-called tribals (*âdivâsi*) who are partly Hinduized, live on the margins of society. Until the status of Untouchable was officially abolished in 1955, all contact with them was forbidden.

In reality, this socio-religious subdivision goes hand-in-hand with one based on socio-professional criteria, involving the vast number of so-called *jâti* (literally "birth"). *Jâti* in turn are made up of sub-groups and generally endogamous lineages, each of which is endowed with hereditary attributes, customs, obligations and prerogatives. In general, an individual identifies primarily with his *jâti* rather than his *varna*: the *jâti* is an extension of his family, and it is within the *jâti* that he establishes the links of solidarity through which – in most cases – he will find a spouse. Therefore, the *jâti* can be compared to the medieval guilds and corporations of the West.

The entire social hierarchy is determined by ideas of relative purity and impurity. Thus, contact with a person belonging to a lower caste is considered to be polluting by people belonging to the higher castes, in varying degrees depending on the extent of the hierarchical gap. Note that in its Western usage, the term "caste", which refers to both *varna* and *jâti*, derives from the Portuguese *casto*, which indeed means "pure".

It is also worth noting that the social hierarchy does not coincide either with a hierarchy of political power or with one based on economic wealth. Castes are not equivalent to what we mean by social classes. The now dethroned kings and princes are *kshatriya* and therefore hierarchically inferior to Brahmans whose prerogatives are restricted to the doctrinal science and the practice of Vedic sacrifice. As to wealth, it derives from the professional attributes of a community and the potential skills of its members rather than the individual's place in the social order. Material wealth is not a criterion that determines hierarchy.

Each caste has its own code of conduct, and its rank is mainly determined by obligations (food, sexual, ritual, etc.) and prohibitions imposed on its members. In general, the higher the caste in the hierarchy, the more numerous the obligations and the stricter the prohibitions its members are subjected to. Finally, if the caste principle is common across India, each region has developed its own interpretation, as well as its own subdivision according to the circumstances and the special needs of its population.

Contrary to conventional wisdom, the principal question currently raised by the persistence of the caste system focuses on the better defence of each community's interests rather than on the abolition of the system as such. In any case, caste solidarity remains a pillar of the social structure. Meeting the economic challenges of modern society requires the establishment of farmers' and artisans' cooperatives at local level and a better distribution network for their products. It also requires growing professional diversification, for the hereditary attributes of each individual may no longer allow him to satisfy the material needs of his family.

Caste membership – whatever the caste – is rarely brought into question. It is accepted and at the same time proudly proclaimed, even by the most disadvantaged groups and the most fervent members of the Communist party. Paradoxically, the few who openly contest the caste principle are often Brahmans. Otherwise, whatever their lineage, people are generally proud of their condition. The system justifies the individual's existence, accords it meaning and dignity, and at the same time links him via the appropriate myth to a prestigious origin that is always regarded as defying comparison!

In reality if not always in political discourse, present-day Kerala has to a large extent kept up the caste system, including the social organisation, division of labour and prohibitions that derive from it. Power is no longer held systematically by the reigning castes since these have been dethroned in favour of a system based on democracy. But though Kerala has opened up to the modern world and the market economy, its religious life continues to be governed by the principle of dividing up the required tasks among hereditary groups of specialists.

Since India gained independence in 1947, the situation has nevertheless changed considerably, especially after the abolition of the feudal system in 1964. For centuries, most arts and rituals in Kerala evolved in the context of an oligarchy. They were either directly linked to service at the princely courts or the latter had encouraged their practice by constant patronage. For many landowners, it was a question of honour to support a community or family of artists by allotting them a paddy or a piece of land for their subsistence, or by providing direct economic assistance that would allow the group to make, buy or maintain the resources necessary to carry out its art.

The colonial authorities were generally tolerant of, or indifferent to, these traditions in which they saw no direct risk since these did not affect their political power and their stranglehold over external trade. They viewed them either as being part of the private sphere of their subjects or as manifestations of a form of heathenism that, though to be condemned in principle, was regarded as inoffensive.

Faced with drastic economic constraints, modern India was not in a position to take over the ancient political structures. Though new social and economic dynamics were introduced by land reform and the abolition of ancestral privileges, these came at a price, since they led to the impoverishment and sometimes even the disappearance of many occupational activities dating back to the old regime. The most adversely affected were the various occupations linked directly to service at the temples, for which there seemed to be no viable alternative under the new circumstances.

"Most of the problems experienced nowadays by artisans and artists dependent on the shrines started after India gained independence", we were told by our friend Ravi; "these people were dispossessed of the land they had been entrusted with and from which they drew most of their subsistence, and they lost the patronage of the patrician families that had provided them with a decent and regular income. Now they barely have anything left. Badly paid, they must also pay exorbitant taxes".

To survive, artists (musicians, dancers, actors, etc.) have started to diversify by adapting the services they usually render to the challenges of the modern world. The wisest among them have put their talents into the hands of the tourist industry or of the numerous regional radio or television stations. However, this most interesting choice requires that they accept the rules of the game, namely, by offering a smooth and unobjectionable version of their art, formulated to meet the demands of the new patrons.

Although this contributes to some extent to preserving appearances, it is not a solution. To uphold ancestral rituals in a changing world, new strategies are needed, based on a lucid appraisal of the situation and its social and economic consequences. Thus, the organisation of the large yearly village festivals is now in the hands of committees of notables belonging to the new rural "middle classes" who have taken over in part from the old reigning families, though without having the economic means traditionally owned by the former.

This development has led to changes in the organisation of the ceremonies. Their past splendour was possible only because of the availability of extensive funds. To remain impressive – the organisation of a ritual is expensive – the present-day officials must come up with solutions that guarantee these events will bring in enough money. To attract the crowds, some Keralan religious ceremonies have thus been transformed into fairground festivals, with their numbers, variety shows and modern features meant to attract youngsters in search of a Bollywood type of entertainment. But with a few rare exceptions, this effervescence does not infringe upon the sphere of the sacred. Rather than proscribing the presence of the profane, the sphere of the sacred tends to absorb it, for the exultation of the senses is part and parcel of its stratagems of seduction.

Various lucrative activities, some more invasive than others, have mushroomed on the margins of the rituals proper. Often the shrines are surrounded by all kinds of stalls: herbalists, astrologers, fortune-tellers, tattooers and small itinerant vendors, one booth more enticing than the next. Having become key players at most of the rituals, the pedlars of the temple never miss an occasion to be present where the gods manifest themselves!

The photographs of Johnathan Watts both plunge us into the magic universe of the rituals of Kerala and relate his personal voyage through the maze of a complex and paradoxical society, one drawn between the demands of a forceful tradition and the attractions of a rather chaotic modernity. Above all, they tell a love story between the photographer and the "small nothings" of a captivating universe – a universe reflected in the writings of Arundhati Roy who stigmatised its shortcomings with all the tenderness and ferocity of her devastating talent.

The quality of Johnathan Watts' photography is simply obvious, for it contains the mix of thoroughness and sensibility characteristic of the real artist. His images do not describe, they fill our vision. With humour and empathy, they invite us to share in a life experience. They show us a humble and hard-working people who are manifestly inhabited by the fire of a particular grace. When all is said and done, it is this fire, this light that guides us through the pages and forms the essential message of this beautiful volume.

A Shared Viewpoint

Johnathan Watts

India is a complex and often difficult environment within which to work. It is easy to be seduced by the spectacular quality of everyday life. It is a myriad of activities and the senses are assaulted by its bustling markets and colourful peoples, its spicy cuisine and exotic perfumes, its magnificent architecture and beautiful landscapes. However, under this stimulating exterior there exists a country in perpetual conflict with itself, a society of extremes, of contrasts, caught between tradition and modernity, reality and myth, good and evil, between pacifism and uncontrollable violence, incessant noise and profound silence. The southern State of Kerala is a perfect example of this extraordinary mixture.

Known by its inhabitants as "Gods' Own Land", Kerala is renowned for its independent character, its diversity of religions, its spice trade, its splendid coastline and its innumerable rituals. The Communist party has always been in power, losing elections for the first time only in 2003. Kerala is also known for its legion of workers' syndicates. Political rallies, strikes and demonstrations are a regular, almost daily occurrence and the red colour of the Communist party dominates the urban landscape in the form of flags, posters and graffiti. It claims to have the highest literacy level of any state in India (97%) and bookshops and newspaper stands thrive among the busy *tchaï* stalls. Painted Hindu temples, Christian churches and Islamic mosques can be seen almost side by side, a strong reminder of the religious tolerance of this southern state. Hindu temple music can be heard emanating from rusty loudspeakers, blending in with the call to prayer from an adjacent mosque.

The people of Kerala live in a paradise, a Garden of Eden, dominated by a tropical climate and under a canopy of luxuriant, saturating greens. A colour which, surprisingly, I never saw used in the make-up or the costumes of the village rituals that I saw.

It is here, amongst these modest communities, that one discovers another India, a different, more private world that lies beneath the coconut plantations and muddy rice fields. Simple, naive village folk reveal a certain vulnerability to their daily lives. Religious and social taboos are more defined and the differences in castes more obvious. Curious and sometimes a little suspicious of outsiders, these villagers were magnanimous in their attitude towards us and magnificent in their beliefs.

I was accompanied by Laurent Aubert, an ethnomusicologist from the Ethnographic Museum of Geneva, and Ravi Gopalan Nair, a friend, artist, coordinator, and specialist on Keralan rituals. We were a multidisciplinary team. We had been sent by the Museum to document some of these annual festivals and we returned in 1999 with numerous sound recordings, films, photographs and objects to add to its collection. We also returned with a proposition for a future exhibition on Keralan rituals to be held in Geneva. This proposition was accepted by the Museum and resulted in a second mission in 2001. Over the course of these two missions we recorded 73 hours of music, 83 hours of film and took more than 7000 photographs. We also acquired for the Museum's collection numerous objects, costumes, headdresses, and statues.

In 2002, more than one year after returning from the second field mission, I was asked to make a preliminary selection of photographs with the eventual goal of publishing a book. It might have seemed a rather daunting task to choose a hundred or so images from several thousand colour and black-and-white photographs, but strangely enough the choice was made without too much hesitation. A natural selection and a certain rhythm quickly became apparent even though, since the first trip in 1998–99, I had spent very little time studying the documentation that we had brought back. Perhaps this "distance" meant that I had a fresh view on the collection of photographs of Kerala and that my choice was inspired by rediscovering and, in a way, reliving the rituals and experiences that I had witnessed. But I do not believe this to be so. Remarkably the "maquette" varies very little in content, rhythm and meaning from, this, the final product. Or is this so remarkable? With hindsight, I am now aware that the influences and emotions while photographing in the field had in fact consciously or unconsciously destined this final choice. This may seem more than a little obvious now, but I was not fully aware of any precise structure or coherence to my work at the time.

The diversity and number of temple festivals and rituals held each year are almost incalculable but they mirror the social and cultural richness that is Kerala. These annual events help to consolidate both village society and the family unit. They respond to both collective and individual concerns, such as prosperous harvests, the danger of epidemics, or, more personally, financial or fertility problems. By communicating directly with their gods within the confines of their sanctuaries and in a joyous and festive manner, both the earthly and spiritual needs of the villagers are met. In this way, the communities also guard and protect their own identities. The attendance at these rituals can vary from only several hundred people to up to 20,000 or more, depending on the size of the village and the importance of the temple within the district.

To arrive in a village in full festivity, often when the ritual has already begun and often at night, is a confusing and disorientating experience. We had to adjust to its geography, its mood and its public, and respond accordingly. We were concerned and even a little stressed not to disturb the harmony of the proceedings (even though that was inevitable) or at least to do so as little as possible. Also we did not want to upset a ceremony by an unintentional mal-address. These thoughts and emotions were predominant in conditioning our behaviour even before actually beginning work. Each village was different and each performance (whether the same ritual or not) was practised to its own unique rhythm in front of its own unique public and we had to adapt to these changes so as to capture the significance and importance of each individual presentation.

Seeing these rituals for the first time I was unable to anticipate the key moments and that meant that I had to work instinctively and therefore develop an immediate rapport with what was unfolding before the camera. Intuition plays a major role in such circumstances. Sometimes many different aspects of a ritual were being performed simultaneously in other parts of the village, so decisions had to be made quickly and instinctively as to what to cover and what to ignore. So, consciously or not, one actively starts to make a personal choice or selection of the events taking place before the camera. Not understanding what we were seeing and not working to any definite brief meant that there was a tendency to "over-document". Everything and anything was and could be important or useful in the future. This attitude was more pronounced during the first field mission as we had little experience of what to expect and of what we wanted to record.

During the 1998–99 trip I was not aware of the very complex choreography to these rituals. Everything seemed to be extremely chaotic and haphazard, a strong image prevailed of a lack of organisation giving the impression that improvisation from both the artists and the public alike was the order to these festivities. In fact this impression could not have been further from the truth. Inevitably we were seduced by the spectacular. It was difficult, especially during the first mission, to focus on or even pay much attention to the more discreet gestures and acts which were also an integral part of these rituals. The quantity of photographs and films taken are a testament to the strong physical and emotional reactions we had to the scenes where silver-fanged gods, in extraordinary costumes and adorned with immense headdresses, were literally set alight during the darkest hours of a Keralan night.

Many rituals, often mobilising entire villages, were in fact extremely well organised and very precise with their presentations and timing. Their natural rhythm can be compared to that of the day and night and even to the greater cycle of life itself. The beginning of a ritual was often slow. Movements were unhurried, almost lethargic, like early morning risers before dawn. Oil lamps are lit, and floors are swept to the gentle drumming of *chenda* announcing the "birth" or beginning of the proceedings. In this way the Ancestor Gods are evoked and villagers leave their daily tasks and make their unhurried way to the shrine. After this introduction comes the "adolescent" stage, a certain energy and dynamism become apparent, and the gods are often represented in their immature or youthful states; there was sometimes a lot of interaction and even playfulness with the young section of the public. Following this, and often in the middle of the night, the gods appear in their "mature" forms, frightening and authoritative. The dance rhythms are at their most vigorous and energetic, the music and the drumming reaching a crescendo, firebrands adding even more atmosphere to this most dramatic part of the ceremony. Towards dawn, a more leisurely pace returns to the proceedings, the wisdom and importance of "old age" leading the ritual to a gentle and calm conclusion.

All the photographs, both colour and black-and-white, were taken on traditional film and not with a digital camera. So several weeks and hundreds of photographs later, a certain state of anguish prevailed. All the images were "phantom" photographs; as yet no film had been developed. The photographer cannot go back and retake failed pictures like a writer can rewrite a sentence. This means that the "traditional" photographer has to remain extremely concentrated, the adrenaline of "shooting blind" focusing all his energies while often working in conditions that are not always ideal. Photographing with this uncertainty, and later the pleasure and disappointments in viewing the results, sometimes unexpected, is the beauty and the magic of the photographic medium.

Out of respect for the public and by not forgetting that these rituals are essentially religious events, it was also necessary to find the right balance between being not too "aggressive" in taking photographs or too "timid" and running the risk of missing images altogether. Sometimes I decided to refrain from taking pictures completely, remaining purely a spectator. These were often during very intimate moments when, perhaps, a distressed local was seeking guidance or blessings from his or her god, for personal or family reasons, or, when, overcome by the events, someone fainted or entered into a trance. Often many of these emotionally charged scenes do not photograph as well as one might imagine. The build-up of tension and the degree of collective emotions are sometimes lost in the translation to film. Many of the photographs were taken at night using flash lighting, and this did not help in rendering the photographer discreet.

There were also extraordinary contrasts. Firebrands with their warm and atmospheric light counterbalanced the cold linear neon tubes that were attached to trees and buildings in and around the sanctuaries. Traditional singing and rhythmic, light drumming could be heard playing to the background sound of the distant throbbing of electric generators. Garish plastic dolls were for sale on festival stalls near intricately carved stone statues of gods, decorated with orange turmeric powder and garlanded with flowers. All these contrasts mirrored, on a smaller scale, what makes India so interesting.

Kerala was a rare and exceptional experience for me both professionally and personally. During the time spent working and travelling, I developed an enormous respect and friendship for my two companions. But Kerala does not remain just a collection of photographs or a series of distant memories of brief but intense meetings with simple villagers celebrating their devotional faith. Neither does it remain an exclusive privilege to have been accepted into the very closed and secret domain of the sacred and the profane, where the spiritual and earthly worlds are unified and where men are transformed into gods. It was all of these things and more, much more.

The following 120 photographs represent only about 1 1/2 seconds of real time from more than 4 months spent in the field, yet almost all of my experiences of the rituals of Kerala are, in one form or another, represented in *Kerala, of Gods and Men*.

Manifestation du parti communiste,
au pouvoir dans l'État du Kerala
jusqu'en 2003. Calicut (Kozhikode),
février 2001.

A political rally of the Communist
party, in power until 2003 in the
State of Kerala. Calicut (Kozhikode),
February 2001.

Le rickshaw est toujours un moyen très
populaire de se déplacer dans les rues
bondées de l'Inde. Calicut.

The rickshaw is still an ideal means
of getting around in the congested
streets of India. Calicut.

En Inde, chaque mouvement est un geste artistique. Vendeur de thé *tchaï*. Trivandrum (Thiruvananthapuram).

Throughout India every gesture is that of an artist. *Tchaï wallah (tea* seller). Trivandrum (Thiruvananthapuram).

Pieds nus et étouffés par la chaleur, les ouvriers coulent le métal fondu dans de grands moules destinés à la fabrication des lampes de temple. Usine Bellwicks Bellmetal. Irinjalakuda, district de Thrissur.

Bare footed and suffocating from the heat, workers are seen pouring liquid metal into moulds used for making temple lamps. Bellwicks Bellmetal Society. Irinjalakuda, district of Thrissur.

Une fois refroidi, le moulage est
façonné et décoré sur un tour manuel.
Usine Bellwicks Bellmetal. Irinjalakuda,
district de Thrissur.

Once cooled, the lamp is turned
on a manual lathe. Bellwicks
Bellmetal Society. Irinjalakuda,
district of Thrissur.

L'absurdité d'une affiche vantant des vêtements citadins au milieu de la campagne profonde. District de Trivandrum.

The absurdity of an advertising hording promoting "city" shirts in the middle of the countryside. District of Trivandrum.

L'image de l'homme moderne
occidentalisé domine le paysage
urbain. Cochin (Kochi), district
d'Ernakulam.

The image of a modern westernised
man dominates the city landscape.
Cochin (Kochi), district of Ernakulam.

Chapeaux de paille destinés aux touristes. Marché des antiquaires du quartier juif de Mattancherrey, Cochin.

Straw hats on sale for tourists in the antiques market of the old Jewish quarter of Mattancherrey. Cochin.

Jeu d'ombre et de lumière
dans les palmes, matière naturelle
omniprésente dans la vie quotidienne,
de la confection des nattes et paniers
aux costumes des rituels.

Light and shadows in the palm leaves.
Natural fibres are used in everyday life,
from the making of baskets and mats
to ritual costumes and accessories.

Le climat paradisiaque du Kerala
permet trois récoltes de riz par année.
Et pourtant, de nombreux rituels ont
pour but de favoriser la fertilité et
l'abondance des récoltes.

The favourable climate allows
for up to three rice harvests a year.
Nevertheless, numerous village
rituals pray for annual prosperity
and fertility.

Les musiciens, en tête du cortège
parti chercher de l'eau bénite dans
un temple brahmanique proche,
s'arrêtent dans chaque village traversé
pour annoncer le début du rituel.
Village de Tenjippalam, district de
Malappuram.

Musicians, at the head of a procession
in search of purified water at a
neighbouring Brahmin shrine, visit
each village on the way announcing
the beginning of a ritual. Tenjippalam
village, district of Malappuram.

La rigueur de la discipline d'apprentissage se lit dans le regard de ce garçon à l'écoute de son maître. Théâtre rituel de Krishnâttam. Natana Kairali Institute, Irinjalakuda, district de Thrissur.

The rigour of the discipline of learning can be seen in the look of this young boy. The dance-drama of Krishnâttam. Natana Kairali Institute, Irinjalakuda, district of Thrissur.

Village de Perumanna, district de Calicut.

Perumanna village, district of Calicut.

Les festivités débordent le cadre du temple ; les vendeurs ambulants attirés par les célébrations installent leur stand de pacotille. Temple de Chîni Kanâri Bhagavatî, village de Tenjippalam, district de Malappuram.

Festivities overflow the temple boundary ; travelling salesmen set up their stalls around the sanctuary. Temple of Chîni Kanâri Bhagavatî. Tenjippalam village, district of Malappuram.

Paré de ses grelots et sonnailles de chevilles, un danseur de Teyyam attend de revêtir son costume. Temple de Putiya Bhagavatî, village de Mullûl, district de Kannur.

The feet of a Teyyam dancer adorned with jingles. The artist is waiting patiently for his turn to be dressed. Temple of Putiya Bhagavatî. Mullûl village, district of Kannur.

Le «tracé de l'aire» (*kalam ezhuttu*), dessin en poudres colorées représentant la déesse Bhadrakâlî, en prélude au rituel du Mutiyêttu. Temple d'Ellu Manakkal Bhagavatî, village d'Erûr, district d'Ernakulam.

An image drawn with coloured powders, *kalam ezhuttu*, representing the goddess Badrakâlî, a preliminary to the ritual of Mutiyêttu. Temple of Ellu Manakkal Bhagavatî. Erûr village, district of Ernakulam.

Lecteurs matinaux dans un débit
de *tchaï* (thé). L'État du Kerala est l'un
des plus alphabétisés de l'Inde. Village
de Kûnathara, district de Palakkad.

Early risers in a *tchaï* shop. Kerala
claims to be the most literate State
in India. Kûnathara village, district
of Palakkad.

À l'ombre de son éléphant décoré,
le cornac attend le début de la
procession rituelle. Festival d'Edappal.
Temple de Kulangara Bhagavatî,
village de Shukapuram, district
de Malappuram.

Under the protective arch of his
decorated elephant, a mahout waits
for the ritual to begin. Festival
of Edappal. Temple of Kulangara
Bhagavatî. Shukapuram village,
district of Malappuram.

Le temple de Shri Nâgarâja est l'un des plus anciens sanctuaires du Kerala dédiés au culte des dieux-serpents (*nâga*). Un tableau dans l'entrée donne l'impression que l'ancienne Mère sainte est encore présente. Temple de Mannarasala, district d'Alappuzha.

One of the oldest in Kerala, the Temple of Shri Nâgarâja is dedicated to the cult of the snake gods (*nâga*). A painting left in the doorway gives the impression of a ghostly return of the deceased Mother of the temple. Temple of Mannarasala, district of Alappuzha.

Lors d'un rituel de Tirayâttam,
un fidèle possédé par l'esprit d'un
serpent jette une poudre rouge sur
l'autel de Nâgakâli, la déesse aux
serpents. Temple de Chettipurakandi
Bhagavatî, village de Putiyapalam,
district de Calicut.

During the ritual of Tirayâttam,
a devotee, possessed by the snake
spirit, spits out a red powder onto the
altar of Nâgakâli the snake goddess.
Temple of Chettipurakandi Bhagavatî.
Putiyapalam village, district of Calicut.

Procession du Kalasam. Précédés des musiciens, les médiums (*velichappad*) entrent dans l'enceinte du temple en brandissant leur sabre sacré. Temple de Chettipurakandi Bhagavatî, village de Putiyapalam, district de Calicut.

Kalasam, the procession of temple mediums (*velichappad*) carrying ritual swords enters the sanctuary accompanied by musicians. Temple of Chettipurakandi Bhagavatî, Putiyapalam village, district of Calicut.

Joueurs de tambours *chenda* lors d'un rituel de Teyyam. Temple de Muchilôttu Bhagavatî, village de Narath, district de Kannur.

Chenda drummers during a Teyyam ritual. Temple of Muchilôttu Bhagavatî, Narath village, district of Kannur.

Procession du Kalasam :
les *velichappad* (mediums)
ramènent l'eau sacrée au sanctuaire.
Village de Tenjippalam, district
de Malappuram.

Kalasam, the procession of the
velichappad (mediums) returning
to the sanctuary carrying sacred water.
Tenjippalam village, district of
Malappuram.

Abrité du soleil, un brahmane
accomplit son offrande (*pûja*). Temple
de Chîni Kanâri Bhagavatî, village de
Tenjippalam, district de Malappuram.

Shaded from the sun, a Brahmin priest
prepares offerings (*pûja*). Temple of
Chîni Kanâri Bhagavatî. Tenjippalam
village, district of Malappuram.

Deux personnages Rudramâlan
en train de se faire maquiller dans
la loge des artistes, «la pièce verte»,
édifiée en feuilles de palme. Préparation
du rituel de Tirayâttam, la «danse de la
splendeur». Sanctuaire de Chîni Kanâri
Bhagavati, village de Tenjippalam,
district de Malappuram.

Preparation and make up of two
characters Rudramâlan in the "green
room", a temporary structure built
to house the artists. The ritual of
Tirayâttam "dance of the splendour".
Temple of Chîni Kanâri Bhagavatî.
Tenjippalam village, district
of Malappuram.

Rite d'offrande (*pûja*) effectué par
Rameshan pour faciliter le bon
déroulement du rituel de Tirayâttam.
Temple de Chettipurakandi Bhagavatî,
village de Putiyapalam, district de Calicut.

Rameshan performing a *pûja* as a
prayer for the smooth performance
of a Tirayâttam ritual. Temple
of Chettipurakandi Bhagavatî.
Putiyapalam village, district of Calicut.

La loge des artistes est consacrée et le
public ne peut y pénétrer. Préparation
et maquillage d'un danseur de Teyyam.
Temple de Putiya Bhagavatî, village de
Mullûl, district de Kannur.

The artists' lodge is sacred. The
preparation and make-up of a
performer for a Teyyam ritual. Temple
of Putiya Bhagavatî. Mullûl village,
district of Kannur.

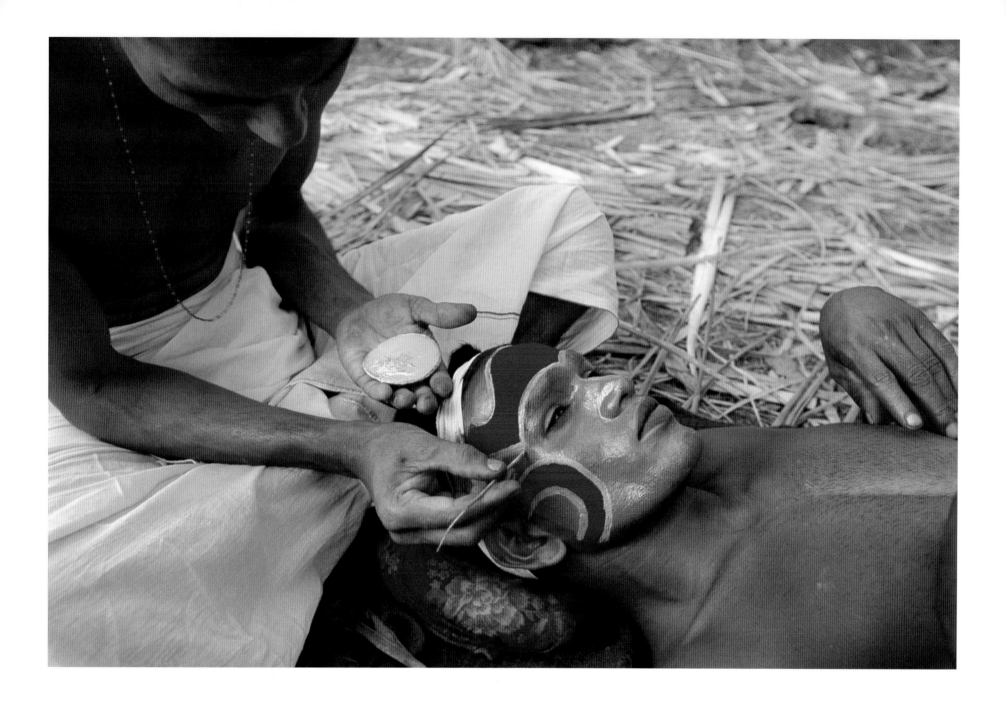

On applique le maquillage à l'aide
d'une fine tige de palmier à l'extrémité
taillée en pinceau. Rituel de Teyyam.
Temple de Putiya Bhagavatî, village de
Mullûl, district de Kannur.

The make-up is applied with a thin
cane twig which is bitten repeatedly
at one end to create a makeshift brush.
Teyyam ritual. Temple of Putiya Bhagavatî.
Mullûl village, district of Kannur.

Préparation d'un jeune acteur pour le théâtre rituel Krishnâttam. Sur le fond de couleur jaune, l'artiste mélange du rouge pour produire un orangé du plus bel effet, avant le maquillage final appliqué par les maquilleurs spécialisés. Natana Kairali Institute, Irinjalakuda, district de Thrissur.

Preparation of a young actor for the dance-drama of Krishnâttam. The red is mixed with the yellow base to create a strong orange before the more intricate work is applied by specialized make-up artists. Natana Kairali Institute, Irinjalakuda, district of Thrissur.

L'acteur incarnant le démon Dârikan
dans le rituel du Mutiyêttu met la
touche finale à son maquillage. Temple
d'Ellu Manakkal Bhagavatî, village d'Erûr,
district d'Ernakulam.

The demon Dârikan adds the
finishing touch to his face make-up.
Mutiyêttu ritual. Temple of Ellu
Manakkal Bhagavatî. Erûr village,
district of Ernakulam.

Rituel de Tirayâttam. Les bandes
de coton enroulées autour de la taille
du danseur sont comme une
superposition de jupons virevoltant
pendant la performance. Temple
de Chettipurakandi Bhagavatî, village
de Putiyapalam, district de Calicut.

Tirayâttam ritual. Meters of cotton
are wound around the waist
to give the effect of billowing
skirts. Temple of Chettipurakandi
Bhagavatî. Putiyapalam village,
district of Calicut.

Rituel de Tirayàttam. Indifférent
aux bruits qui l'entourent, l'artiste se
concentre pour interpréter le rôle de
Bhandâramûrtti, ancêtre féminin de la
communauté villageoise. Temple de
Chettipurakandi Bhagavatî, village de
Putiyapalam, district de Calicut.

Tirayàttam ritual. An artist representing
the ancestor goddess Bhandâramûrtti
is enveloped in another world.
Temple of Chettipurakandi
Bhagavatî. Putiyapalam village,
district of Calicut.

Les deux personnages représentant
le dieu Rudramahâlan au cours
d'un rituel de Tirayâttam. Temple
de Chîni Kanâri Bhagavatî, village de
Tenjippalam, district de Malappuram.

Two characters representing the god
Rudramahâlan during a Tirayâttam
ritual. Temple of Chîni Kanâri Bhagavatî.
Tenjippalam village, district of
Malappuram.

Le maquillage extraordinaire d'un danseur de Teyyam, la «danse des dieux». Temple de Putiya Bhagavatî, village de Mullûl, district de Kannur.

The exquisite make-up of a Teyyam. Teyyam ritual, "dance of the Gods". Temple of Putiya Bhagavatî. Mullûl village, district of Kannur.

Le faste des couleurs de la déesse
Bhandâramûrtti contraste avec le bleu
nuit de la bâche en plastique couvrant
la loge des artistes. Rituel de Tirayâttam.
Temple de Chettipurakandi Bhagavatî,
village de Putiyapalam, district de Calicut.

The auspicious colours of the
goddess Bhandâramûrtti contrast
with the blue of a false night created
by the plastic sheeting used for
a makeshift roof. Tirayâttam ritual.
Temple of Chettipurakandi Bhagavatî.
Putiyapalam village, district of Calicut.

La présence de la déesse Bhandâramûrtti investit le regard du danseur au cours d'un rituel de Tirayâttam. Temple de Chettipurakandi Bhagavatî, village de Putiyapalam, district de Calicut.

The presence of the goddess Bhandâramûrtti is revealed in the intense gaze of an artist during a Tirayâttam ritual. Temple of Chettipurakandi Bhagavatî. Putiyapalam village, district of Calicut.

Le héros Kativannûr Vîran lors
d'un rituel de Teyyam. Temple
de Putiya Bhagavatî, village
de Mullûl, district de Kannur.

The hero Kativannûr Vîran during
a Teyyam ritual. Temple of Putiya
Bhagavatî. Mullûl village, district
of Kannur.

Par la magie de son regard, ce danseur reflète la puissance du héros (*vîran*) de Kativannûr. Rituel de Teyyam. Temple de Putiya Bhagavatî, village de Mullûl, district de Kannur.

The power of reincarnating a hero (*vîran*) is reflected in the striking look of this artist. Teyyam ritual. Temple of Putiya Bhagavatî. Mullûl village, district of Kannur.

Le héros Kativannûr Vîran. Les impressionnantes coiffes sont en bois sculpté décoré de tissu et de feuilles de métal coloré. Rituel de Teyyam. Temple de Putiya Bhagavatî, village de Mullûl, district de Kannur.

The hero Kativannûr Vîran. The impressive headdresses are carved from wood and decorated with silver. Teyyam ritual. Temple of Putiya Bhagavatî. Mullûl village, district of Kannur.

Dernières touches de maquillage
de l'acteur avant la performance d'un
rituel de Teyyam. Temple de Putiya
Bhagavatî, village de Mullûl, district
de Kannur.

An actor in deep concentration as the
finishing touches to his make-up is
applied. Teyyam ritual. Temple of Putiya
Bhagavatî. Mullûl village, district
of Kannur.

Aucun détail du costume de Teyyam n'est oublié, même le dos du personnage est très élaboré. Rituel de Teyyam. Temple de Putiya Bhagavatî, village de Mullûl, district de Kannur.

No detail is overlooked, even the back of a Teyyam artist is elaborately decorated. Teyyam ritual. Temple of Putiya Bhagavatî. Mullûl village, district of Kannur.

Bien qu'elles ne participent pas au rituel, les femmes demeurent des spectatrices vigilantes et discrètes du rituel de Tirayâttam. Temple de Chîni Kanâri Bhagavatî, village de Tenjippalam, district de Malappuram.

Although forbidden to participate in the dance, female spectators watch attentively from a good vantage point. Tirayâttam ritual. Temple of Chîni Kanâri Bhagavatî. Tenjippalam village, district of Malappuram.

Impressionnés par la transformation
d'un homme en dieu, un père et son fils
hésitent à s'approcher. Rituel de
Teyyam. Temple de Putiya Bhagavatî,
village de Mullûl, district de Kannur.

Impressed by the change from man
to god, a father and his child hesitate
to approach nearer. Teyyam ritual.
Temple of Putiya Bhagavatî. Mullûl
village, district of Kannur.

Même dans une foule de vingt
ou trente mille personnes, les hommes
restent séparés des femmes. Festival
d'Edappal. Temple de Kulangara
Bhagavatî, village de Shukapuram,
district de Malappuram.

Even in a crowd of 20 to 30,000 people,
a separation between men and women
is apparent. Festival of Edappal. Temple
of Kulangara Bhagavatî. Shukapuram
village, district of Malappuram.

La ceinture de coton rouge portée par ces médiums indique l'importance de leur rôle dans le déroulement du rituel. Temple de Chettipurakandi Bhagavatî, village de Putiyapalam, district de Calicut.

The red cotton belt worn by these temple attendants signifies the importance of the role they play in the ritual proceedings. Temple of Chettipurakandi Bhagavatî. Putiyapalam village, district of Calicut.

Au rythme des tambours, la déesse
Bhandâramûrtti s'avance sur l'aire de
danse au milieu de la foule. Rituel de
Tirayâttam. Temple de Chettipurakandi
Bhagavatî, village de Putiyapalam,
district de Calicut.

Within the sanctuary of the temple,
the goddess Bhandâramûrtti presents
herself to her devotees. Tirayâttam
ritual. Temple of Chettipurakandi
Bhagavatî. Putiyapalam village,
district of Calicut.

La danse de la déesse Bhandâramûrtti.
Rituel de Tirayâttam. Temple de
Chettipurakandi Bhagavatî, village
de Putiyapalam, district de Calicut.

The dance of the goddess
Bhandâramûrtti. Tirayâttam ritual.
Temple of Chettipurakandi Bhagavatî.
Putiyapalam village, district of Calicut.

La danse de la déesse Bhandâramûrtti.
Rituel de Tirayâttam. Temple de
Chettipurakandi Bhagavatî, village
de Putiyapalam, district de Calicut.

The dance of the goddess
Bhandâramûrtti. Tirayâttam ritual.
Temple of Chettipurakandi Bhagavatî.
Putiyapalam village, district of Calicut.

Acteur jouant le rôle de Rudramahâlan, personnage du rituel de Tirayâttam. Temple de Parambath Bhagavatî, village de Tenjippalam, district de Malappuram.

An artist representing the god Rudramahâlan. Tirayâttam ritual. Temple of Parambath Bhagavatî. Tenjippalam village, district of Malappuram.

Un *tira*, personnage fantasmagorique
du rituel de Bhûtanum Tirayum,
la « horde féroce de Kâlî ». Festival
d'Edappal, district de Malappuram.

A *tira*, personage phantasmagoric
during a Bhûtanum Tirayum ritual,
the "ferocious horde of Kâlî". Festival
of Edappal, district of Malappuram.

Jeune officiant au repos devant
les masques d'esprits (*bhûtam*) tirant
la langue. Rituel de Bhûtanum Tirayum.
Village de Karuvanthottil, district
de Palakkad.

A young artist relaxes surrounded
by tongue protruding spirit masks
(*bhûtam*). Bhûtanum Tirayum ritual.
Karuvanthottil village, district
of Palakkad.

Dans l'enceinte d'un temple familial, et sous l'œil attentif des anciens, l'acteur prend garde de ne pas faire choir la lourde coiffe de bois. Rituel de Bhûtanum Tirayum. Village de Karuvanthottil, district de Palakkad.

Under the attentive regard of village elders, a performer has the difficult task of keeping his heavy wooden headdress from unbalancing. Bhûtanum Tirayum ritual. Family Shrine. Karuvanthottil village, district of Palakkad.

Teyyam de l'ancêtre Taypara Dêvata.
Les coiffes de Teyyam peuvent
atteindre jusqu'à huit mètres de haut.
Temple de Putiya Bhagavatî, village
de Mullûl, district de Kannur.

The ancestor god Taypara Dêvata
during a Teyyam ritual. Headdresses
can sometimes reach up to 6 meters
in height. Temple of Putiya Bhagavatî.
Mullûl village, district of Kannur.

Teyyam de l'ancêtre Taypara Dêvata.
Temple de Putiya Bhagavatî, village
de Mullûl, district de Kannur.

The ancestor god Taypara Dêvata
during a Teyyam ritual. Temple
of Putiya Bhagavatî. Mullûl village,
district of Kannur.

Malgré l'ampleur de son costume, le danseur étonne par ses gracieuses évolutions qui peuvent durer des heures. Rituel de Teyyam. Temple de Muchilôttu Bhagavatî, village de Narath, district de Kannur.

Even though hampered by his costume and large headdress, the performer dances for up to several hours. Teyyam ritual. Temple of Muchilôttu Bhagavatî. Narath village, district of Kannur.

Le rituel de Teyyam se termine par
une bénédiction de chaque villageois.
Temple de Muchilôttu Bhagavatî, village
de Narath, district de Kannur.

Teyyam rituals often culminate with a
blessing to each member of the village.
Temple of Muchilôttu Bhagavatî. Narath
village, district of Kannur.

Isolé de son entourage, l'homme-dieu
se recueille. Rituel de Teyyam. Temple
de Putiya Bhagavatî, village de Mullûl,
district de Kannur.

A quiet moment of reflection for
this man-god. Teyyam ritual. Temple
of Putiya Bhagavatî. Mullûl village,
district of Kannur.

Tâlappoli, le cortège des femmes
et des filles portant des offrandes d'eau
purifiée, de riz et de fruits, destinées
à satisfaire la déesse Bhagavatî. Village
de Putiyapalam, district de Calicut.

Tâlappoli, procession of the womenfolk
carrying offerings of fruit, rice and
purified water to a nearby shrine
of Bhagavatî. Putiyapalam village,
district of Calicut.

Tâlappoli, le cortège des femmes. Village
de Putiyapalam, district de Calicut.

Tâlappoli, procession of the women.
Putiyapalam village, district of Calicut.

La foule suit respectueusement le début d'un rituel de Tirayâttam (avec les deux personnages représentant le dieu Rudramahâlan). Temple de Chîni Kanâri Bhagavatî, village de Tenjippalam, district de Malappuram.

The beginning of a Tirayâttam ritual (with the two characters representing the god Rudramahâlan) is watched respectfully by a small crowd. Temple of Chîni Kanâri Bhagavatî. Tenjippalam village, district of Malappuram.

Conscientes des nombreux interdits les concernant, les femmes keralaises se tiennent discrètement à l'écart. Village d'Aranmula, district de Chengannur.

Conscious of the restrictions that society impose upon them, Keralan women are very dignified but extremely discreet. Aranmula village, district of Chengannur.

Nâgakâli, la déesse aux serpents. Rituel
de Tirayâttam. Temple de Parambath
Bhagavatî, village de Tenjippalam,
district de Malappuram.

The goddess Nâgakâli with her
attendants. Tirayâttam ritual. Temple
of Parambath Bhagavatî. Tenjippalam
village, district of Malappuram.

Un médium (*velichappad*) en transe
lors de la procession du Kalasam.
Temple de Chîni Kanâri Bhagavatî,
village de Tenjippalam, district de
Malappuram.

In the Kalasam procession, a
velichappad (medium) in a state
of trance. Temple of Chîni Kanâri
Bhagavatî. Tenjippalam village,
district of Malappuram.

La splendeur des dieux fascine toujours
les jeunes générations. Rituel de
Tirayâttam. Temple de Chettipurakandi
Bhagavatî, village de Putiyapalam,
district de Calicut.

The rituals are also an occasion for the
younger generation to appreciate the
splendour of their gods. Tirayâttam ritual.
Temple of Chettipurakandi Bhagavatî.
Putiyapalam village, district of Calicut.

Jeune public pendant un rituel
de Teyyam. Temple de Kannangâttu
Bhagavatî, village de Narath,
district de Kannur.

A young public during a Teyyam
ritual. Temple of Kannangâttu
Bhagavatî. Narath village, district
of Kannur.

Âsân Madathil Sreedharan Nâyar,
maître de chant du rituel de Patayani
(à gauche), et son frère. Village de
Kottangal, district de Pathanamthitta.

Âsân Madathil Sreedharan Nâyar (left),
master of the singing of Patayani ritual,
seen here with his brother. Kottangal
village, district of Pathanamthitta.

Portrait d'Âsân K.P. Ramakrishnan
Panicker, maître de danse du rituel
de Patayani. Village de Kottangal,
district de Pathanamthitta.

Âsân K.P. Ramakrishnan Panicker, master
of dance of Patayani ritual. Kottangal
village, district of Pathanamthitta.

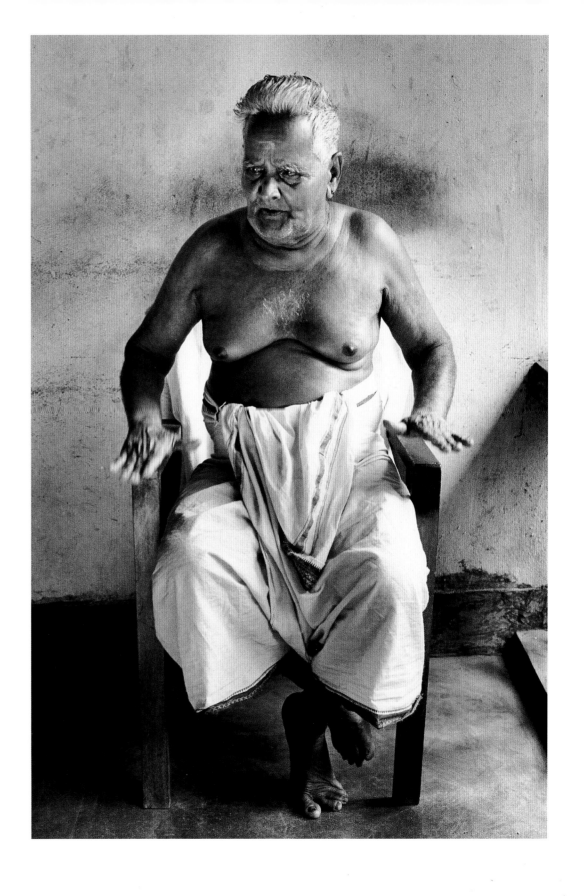

Krishnan Peruvannan, maître de Teyyam. Village d'Azhikkod, district de Kannur.

Krishnan Peruvannan, master of Teyyam ritual. Azhikkod village, district of Kannur.

Portraits de Pazhur Damodhara
Mârâr(†), maître du rituel de Mutiyêttu
et son épouse. Village de Pazhur, district
d'Ernakulam.

Pazhur Damodhara Mârâr(†), master
of Mutiyêttu ritual, with his wife.
Pazhur village, district of Ernakulam.

Portrait de Shri K.L. Krishnankutty Pulavar(†), maître de Tôlpâvakkûttu (théâtre d'ombres). Village de Kûnathara, district de Palakkad.

Shri K.L. Krishnankutty Pulavar(†), master of Tôlpâvakkûttu (shadow puppet theatre). Kûnathara village, district of Palakkad.

Portraits de Shri Appukutty Âsân(†),
maître du rituel de Tirayâttam. Village
de Perumanna, district de Calicut.

Shri Appukutty Âsân(†), master of
Tirayâttam ritual. Perumanna village,
district of Calicut.

Public coloré assistant au rituel de
Tirayâttam. Temple de Chettipurakandi
Bhagavatî, village de Putiyapalam,
district de Calicut.

A colourful public during a Tirayâttam
ritual. Temple of Chettipurakandi
Bhagavatî. Putiyapalam village,
district of Calicut.

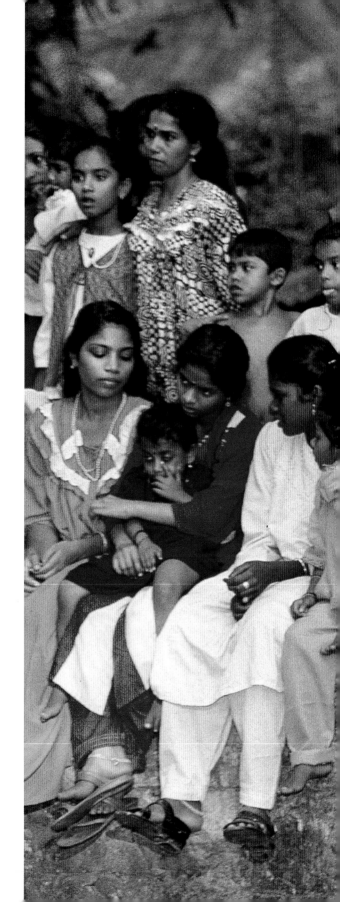

Ouvriers construisant un toit de chaume.
Edappal, district de Malappuram.

Roof workers taking a break. Edappal,
district of Malappuram.

Épouvantail dans le verger d'une
maison pour éloigner les mauvais
esprits. District de Malappuram.

Effigies are often placed around
construction sites to ward off evil
spirits. District of Malappuram.

Les danseurs sont astreints à un
entraînement physique régulier, comme
le Kalarippayattu, l'art martial du Kerala.
École du Hindustan Kalari Sangam,
village de Puthiyara, district de Calicut.

Many actors follow a rigorous
physical training. Kalarippayattu
(martial Arts), School of Hindustan
Kalari Sangam. Puthiyara village,
district of Calicut.

Séance de massage. École du
Hindustan Kalari Sangam, village
de Puthiyara, district de Calicut.

A foot massage. Martial Arts' School
of Hindustan Kalari Sangam. Puthiyara
village, district of Calicut.

Allumage rituel des lampes. Festival
d'Edappal. Temple de Kulangara
Bhagavatî, village de Shukapuram,
district de Malappuram.

The ritual lighting of temple lamps.
Festival of Edappal. Temple of Kulangara
Bhagavatî. Shukapuram village, district
of Malappuram.

Tâlappoli, procession des femmes
devant le temple de Parambath
Bhagavatî. Village de Tenjippalam,
district de Malappuram.

Tâlappoli, procession of women.
Temple of Parambath Bhagavatî.
Tenjippalam village, district
of Malappuram.

Tâlappoli, procession des femmes
autour du temple de la déesse
Pantakkal Parambhu. Village de
Melepattambi, district de Palakkad.

Tâlappoli, procession of women
around the temple of the goddess
Pantakkal Parambhu. Melepattambi
village, district of Palakkad.

Il faut des heures pour tracer ce « tracé de l'aire » (*kalam ezhuttu*), représentant la déesse Bhadrakâlî. Fait de poudres colorées, et après une série d'offrandes *pûja*, ce dessin est ensuite rituellement détruit pour le bienfait des villageois. Temple d'Ellu Manakkal Bhagavatî, village d'Erûr, district d'Ernakulam.

The goddess Bhadrakâlî is here represented by a floor drawing using coloured powders (*kalam ezhuttu*). Having taken around 8 hours to complete and after a lengthy *pûja*, the image is swept into a pile and the powder distributed as an offering to the villagers. Temple of Ellu Manakkal Bhagavatî. Erûr village, district of Ernakulam.

La danse de la déesse Bhandâramûrtti
à la lueur des torches. Rituel de Tirayâttam.
Temple de Chettipurakandi Bhagavatî,
village de Putiyapalam, district de Calicut.

Dance of the goddess
Bhandâramûrtti. Tirayâttam ritual.
Temple of Chettipurakandi Bhagavatî.
Putiyapalam village, district of Calicut.

La danse de la déesse Bhandâramûrtti
à la lueur des torches. Rituel de Tirayâttam.
Temple de Chettipurakandi Bhagavatî,
village de Putiyapalam, district de Calicut.

Dance of the goddess
Bhandâramûrtti. Tirayâttam ritual.
Temple of Chettipurakandi Bhagavatî.
Putiyapalam village, district of Calicut.

Un jongleur et ses boules de feu,
interlude au cours du rituel de Tirayâttam.
Temple de Chettipurakandi Bhagavatî,
village de Putiyapalam, district de Calicut.

Fire acrobats, during an interlude
of a Tirayâttam ritual. Temple
of Chettipurakandi Bhagavatî.
Putiyapalam village, district of Calicut.

La danse de la déesse Bhandâramûrtti.
Rituel de Tirayâttam. Temple de
Chettipurakandi Bhagavatî, village
de Putiyapalam, district de Calicut.

Dance of the goddess
Bhandâramûrtti. Tirayâttam ritual.
Temple of Chettipurakandi Bhagavatî.
Putiyapalam village, district of Calicut.

La danse de la déesse Bhandâramûrtti.
Rituel de Tirayâttam. Temple de
Chettipurakandi Bhagavatî, village
de Putiyapalam, district de Calicut.

Dance of the goddess
Bhandâramûrtti. Tirayâttam ritual.
Temple of Chettipurakandi Bhagavatî.
Putiyapalam village, district of Calicut.

La danse de la déité androgyne
Bhagavatî. Rituel de Tirayâttam. Temple
de Chettipurakandi Bhagavatî, village
de Putiyapalam, district de Calicut.

Dance of the androgynous deity
Bhagavatî. Tirayâttam ritual. Temple
of Chettipurakandi Bhagavatî.
Putiyapalam village, district of Calicut.

Après sa performance, le danseur
incarnant Bhagavatî reçoit les offrandes
des fidèles : des pièces de monnaie
sont appliquées sur son front avant
d'être recueillies dans un panier.
Rituel de Tirayâttam. Temple de
Chettipurakandi Bhagavatî, village
de Putiyapalam, district de Calicut.

When the dance has finished,
the public precipitate to offer
coins which are pressed onto
the forehead of the performer
incarnating Bhagavatî. Tirayâttam
ritual. Temple of Chettipurakandi
Bhagavatî. Putiyapalam village,
district of Calicut.

Le jour va se lever, la jupe en feuilles de bananier du personnage incarnant Rudramahâlan est ornée de torches, tandis qu'il supporte une coiffe de 6-7 mètres de hauteur. Rituel de Tirayâttam. Temple of Chîni Kanâri Bhagavatî, village de Tenjippalam, district de Malappuram.

Just before dawn, an actor playing Rudramahâlan, supporting a headdress of 6 or 7 meters in height, is cocooned in a structure of fresh palm leaves which has been set on fire. Tirayâttam ritual. Temple of Chîni Kanâri Bhagavatî, Tenjippalam village, district of Malappuram.

Les serviteurs du temple, subjugués
par la déesse Putiya Bhagavatî en
flammes. Temple de Putiya Bhagavatî,
village de Mullûl, district de Kannur.

Temple attendants in awe of the blazing
goddess Putiya Bhagavatî. Teyyam ritual.
Temple of Putiya Bhagavatî. Mullûl
village, district of Kannur.

La déesse Putiya Bhagavatî, dont le costume, partiellement détruit par les flammes, est jeté une fois le rituel terminé. Rituel de Teyyam. Temple de Putiya Bhagavatî, village de Mullûl, district de Kannur.

The goddess Putiya Bhagavatî. The costume, partially destroyed by the flames, is discarded after the ritual has finished. Teyyam ritual. Temple of Putiya Bhagavatî. Mullûl village, district of Kannur.

La déesse Putiya Bhagavatî. Rituel de
Teyyam. Temple de Putiya Bhagavatî,
village de Mullûl, district de Kannur.

The goddess Putiya Bhagavatî.
Teyyam ritual. Temple of Putiya Bhagavatî.
Mullûl village, district of Kannur.

Bhairavan, le dieu Shiva représenté par deux personnages simiesques dans le rituel de Tirayâttam. Temple de Chîni Kanâri Bhagavatî. Village de Tenjippalam, district de Malappuram.

Shiva represented by two characters Bhairavan in the form of monkeys. Tirayàttam ritual. Temple of Chîni Kanâri Bhagavatî. Tenjippalam village, district of Malappuram.

Petit lotus (*patmam*) de sables colorés
réalisé sur l'aire sacrée du temple.
Temple de Chîni Kanâri Bhagavatî. Village
de Tenjippalam, district de Malappuram.

Patmam, little lotus, a powdered floor
drawing in front of the altar. Temple
of Chîni Kanâri Bhagavatî. Tenjippalam
village, district of Malappuram.

Le maquillage de Bhadrakâlî dans le rituel de Mutiyêttu représente la variole qui a dévasté des communautés entières autrefois et que seule la déesse a le pouvoir de guérir. Temple d'Ellu Manakkal Bhagavatî, village d'Erûr, district d'Ernakulam.

The heavy face make-up of Bhadrakâlî represents the smallpox disease which devastated entire communities in the past and which only the goddess has the power to eradicate. Mutiyêttu ritual. Temple of Ellu Manakkal Bhagavatî. Erûr village, district of Ernakulam.

Préparation et maquillage des artistes :
le messager des dieux Nâradan et le
démon Dârikan. Rituel du Mutiyêttu :
Temple de Kalampu Kavu Badrakâlî,
village de Pazhur, district d'Ernakulam.

The bearded messenger of the gods,
Nâradan, with the demon Dârikan.
Mutiyêttu ritual. Temple of Kalampu
Kavu Badrakâlî. Pazhur village, district
of Ernakulam.

Le maquillage effrayant de Dârikan dans le rituel du Mutiyêttu. Temple d'Ellu Manakkal Bhagavatî, village d'Erûr, district d'Ernakulam.

The frightening face of Dârikan. Mutiyêttu ritual. Temple of Ellu Manakkal Bhagavatî. Erûr village, district of Ernakulam.

La déesse Nâgakâlî dans le rituel
du Tirayâttam. Temple de Chîni Kanâri
Bhagavatî, village de Tenjippalam,
district de Malappuram.

The goddess Nâgakâlî. Tirayâttam
ritual. Temple of Chîni Kanâri
Bhagavatî. Tenjippalam village,
district of Malappuram.

Le rituel du Mutiyêttu représente
le combat entre Kâlî et Dârikan,
entre le Bien et le Mal, qui voit la
victoire finale de Kâlî. Temple d'Ellu
Manakkal Bhagavatî, village d'Erûr,
district d'Ernakulam.

The ritual of Mutiyêttu tells the story
of the fight between good and evil
(Kâlî and Dârikan) with Kâlî ultimately
triumphing. Temple of Ellu Manakkal
Bhagavatî. Erûr village, district
of Ernakulam.

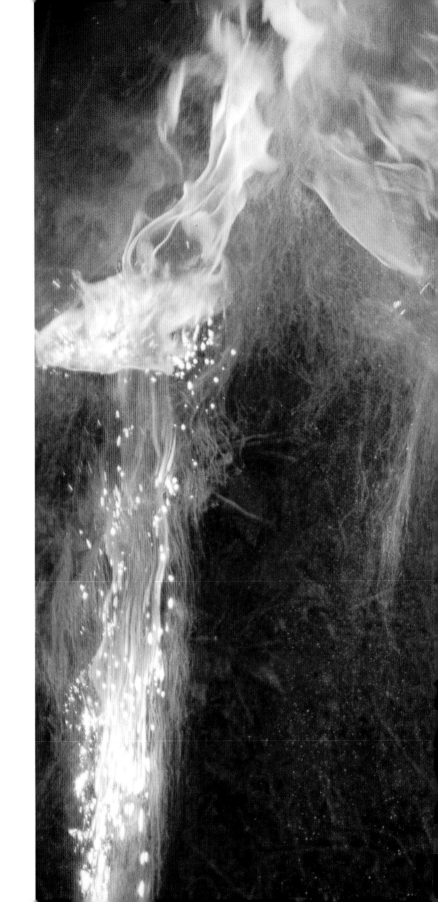

La danse de la déesse Nâgakâli.
Rituel de Tirayâttam. Temple de
Chettipurakandi Bhagavatî, village
de Putiyapalam, district de Calicut.

The goddess Nâgakâli. Tirayâttam ritual.
Temple of Chettipurakandi Bhagavatî.
Putiyapalam village, district of Calicut.

Offrande de riz au personnage
Manakkâtan Gurukkal. Rituel de Teyyam.
Temple de Putiya Bhagavatî, village
de Mullûl, district de Kannur.

An old woman offers a gift of rice
to the character of Manakkâtan
Gurukkal. Teyyam ritual. Temple
of Putiya Bhagavatî, Mullûl village,
district of Kannur.

Les acteurs en transe sont
soigneusement escortés. Rituel de
Teyyam. Temple de Putiya Bhagavatî,
village de Mullûl, district de Kannur.

Actors in a trance are carefully escorted
around the sanctuary. Teyyam ritual.
Temple of Putiya Bhagavatî, Mullûl
village, district of Kannur.

Un assistant du temple finit la transformation du personnage Manakkâtan Gurukkal. Rituel de Teyyam. Temple de Putiya Bhagavatî, village de Mullûl, district de Kannur.

An attendant adds the finishing touches to the character Manakkâtan Gurukkal. Teyyam ritual. Temple of Putiya Bhagavatî. Mullûl village, district of Kannur.

Gênés par la chaleur intense du feu, les percussionnistes doivent chauffer la peau de leurs tambours (*tappu*) pour obtenir le son juste. Rituel de Patayani. Temple de Kottangal Bhagavatî, village de Kottangal, district de Pathanamthitta.

Drummers suffering under the intense heat of a fire. The drums (*tappu*) need to be heated regularly so they stretch and tighten in order to obtain the correct sound. Patayani ritual. Temple of Kottangal Bhagavatî. Kottangal village, district of Pathanamthitta.

La déesse Bhairavî est reconnaissable
au masque (*kôlam*) fait de feuilles
de palme peintes et cousues ensemble
par des fibres. Rituel de Patayani.
Temple de Kottangal, village de
Kottangal, district de Pathanamthitta.

The goddess Bhairavî. The headdresses
(*kôlam*) are made from fresh palm leaves,
sewn together with strips of fibres and
painted. Patayani ritual. Temple of
Kottangal Bhagavatî. Kottangal village,
district of Pathanamthitta.

Tâlappoli, procession des femmes et jeunes filles vêtues de rouge et blanc portant, sur un plateau illuminé par une lampe creusée dans une noix de coco, des offrandes de riz et de fruits. Temple de Chettipurakandi Bhagavatî, village de Putiyapalam, district de Calicut.

Tâlappoli, procession of women and girls all dressed in red and white and carrying makeshift lamps made from coconut shells on a tray containing offerings of fruit and rice. Temple of Chettipurakandi Bhagavati. Putiyapalam village, district of Calicut.

Vingt-et-une lampes à huile sont nécessaires pour illuminer toute la longueur de l'écran. Théâtre d'ombres Tôlpâvakkûttu, par la troupe du maître K.L. Krishnankutty Pulavar. Village de Melepattambi, district de Palakkad.

Twenty-one oil lamps are needed to light the entire length of the screen. Shadow puppet theatre Tôlpâvakkûttu. Troup of the Master K.L. Krishnankutty Pulavar. Melepattambi village, district of Palakkad.

▷▷

Représentation d'un épisode de l'épopée indienne du *Râmayâna*. Les représentations peuvent avoir lieu durant douze nuits consécutives. On voit ici le dieu éléphant Ganapati (Ganesh). Théâtre d'ombres Tôlpâvakkûttu. Village de Melepattambi, district de Palakkad.

The shadow theatre tells stories from the Indian epic the *Râmayâna*. Performances can last up to 12 nights without a pause. Here we see the elephant god Ganapati (Ganesh). Shadow puppet theatre Tôlpâvakkûttu. Melepattambi village, district of Palakkad.